♥ X ♥ X ♥ X ♥

THIS BOOK BELONGS TO:

_____

_____

_____

_____

Want a freebie?!

Email us at
letteringdesignbooks@gmail.com

Title the email "Prayer Journal!" and
we'll send you something fun!

I CALL ON YOU, MY GOD, FOR YOU
WILL ANSWER ME; TURN YOUR EAR
TO ME AND HEAR MY PRAYER.

PSALM 17:6

Today's Verse

Lord teach me to...

I am thankful for...

Prayer Requests

♥ ✗ ♥ ✗ ♥ ✗ ♥

DATE

Today's Verse

Lord teach me to...

I am thankful for...

Prayer Requests

Today's Verse

Lord teach me to...

I am thankful for...

Prayer Requests

❤ X ❤ X ❤ X ❤

DATE

Today's Verse

Lord teach me to...

I am thankful for...

Prayer Requests

Today's Verse

Lord teach me to...

I am thankful for...

Prayer Requests

♥ X ♥ X ♥ X ♥

Today's Verse

Lord teach me to...

I am thankful for...

Prayer Requests

Today's Verse

Lord teach me to...

I am thankful for...

Prayer Requests

♥ X ♥ X ♥ X ♥

DATE

Today's Verse

Lord teach me to...

I am thankful for...

Prayer Requests

Today's Verse

Lord teach me to...

I am thankful for...

Prayer Requests

DATE

Today's Verse

Lord teach me to...

I am thankful for...

Prayer Requests

Today's Verse

Lord teach me to...

I am thankful for...

Prayer Requests

DATE

Today's Verse

Lord teach me to...

I am thankful for...

Prayer Requests

DATE

Today's Verse

Lord teach me to...

I am thankful for...

Prayer Requests

Today's Verse

Lord teach me to...

I am thankful for...

Prayer Requests

♥ ✗ ♥ ✗ ♥ ✗ ♥

Today's Verse

Lord teach me to...

I am thankful for...

Prayer Requests

Today's Verse

Lord teach me to...

I am thankful for...

Prayer Requests

❤✕❤ ✕ ❤✕❤

DATE

Today's Verse

Lord teach me to...

I am thankful for...

Prayer Requests

Today's Verse

Lord teach me to...

I am thankful for...

Prayer Requests

♥✕♥✕♥✕♥

DATE

Today's Verse

Lord teach me to...

I am thankful for...

Prayer Requests

Today's Verse

Lord teach me to...

I am thankful for...

Prayer Requests

♥ X ♥ X ♥ X ♥

DATE

Today's Verse

Lord teach me to...

I am thankful for...

Prayer Requests

Today's Verse

Lord teach me to...

I am thankful for...

Prayer Requests

♥ ✗ ♥ ✗ ♥ ✗ ♥

Today's Verse

Lord teach me to...

I am thankful for...

Prayer Requests

♥ ✗ ♥ ✗ ♥ ✗ ♥

Today's Verse

Lord teach me to...

I am thankful for...

Prayer Requests

Today's Verse

Lord teach me to...

I am thankful for...

Prayer Requests

❤ ✗ ❤ ✗ ❤ ✗ ❤

DATE

Today's Verse

Lord teach me to...

I am thankful for...

Prayer Requests

Today's Verse

Lord teach me to...

I am thankful for...

Prayer Requests

♥ X ♥ X ♥ X ♥

Today's Verse

Lord teach me to...

I am thankful for...

Prayer Requests

Today's Verse

Lord teach me to...

I am thankful for...

Prayer Requests

♥ X ♥ X ♥ X ♥

DATE

Today's Verse

Lord teach me to...

I am thankful for...

Prayer Requests

Today's Verse

Lord teach me to...

I am thankful for...

Prayer Requests

❤ X ❤ X ❤ X ❤

DATE

Today's Verse

Lord teach me to...

I am thankful for...

Prayer Requests

DATE

Today's Verse

Lord teach me to...

I am thankful for...

Prayer Requests

Today's Verse

Lord teach me to...

I am thankful for...

Prayer Requests

♥X♥ X ♥X♥

DATE

Today's Verse

Lord teach me to...

I am thankful for...

Prayer Requests

Today's Verse

Lord teach me to...

I am thankful for...

Prayer Requests

DATE

Today's Verse

Lord teach me to...

I am thankful for...

Prayer Requests

Today's Verse

Lord teach me to...

I am thankful for...

Prayer Requests

Today's Verse

Lord teach me to...

I am thankful for...

Prayer Requests

DATE

Today's Verse

Lord teach me to...

I am thankful for...

Prayer Requests

❤ ✕ ❤ ✕ ❤ ✕ ❤

DATE

Today's Verse

Lord teach me to...

I am thankful for...

Prayer Requests

Today's Verse

Lord teach me to...

I am thankful for...

Prayer Requests

DATE

Today's Verse

Lord teach me to...

I am thankful for...

Prayer Requests

Today's Verse

Lord teach me to...

I am thankful for...

Prayer Requests

DATE

Today's Verse

Lord teach me to...

I am thankful for...

Prayer Requests

Today's Verse

Lord teach me to...

I am thankful for...

Prayer Requests

BE still AND KNOW

Today's Verse

Lord teach me to...

I am thankful for...

Prayer Requests

Today's Verse

Lord teach me to...

I am thankful for...

Prayer Requests

Today's Verse

Lord teach me to...

I am thankful for...

Prayer Requests

Today's Verse

Lord teach me to...

I am thankful for...

Prayer Requests

Today's Verse

Lord teach me to...

I am thankful for...

Prayer Requests

DATE

Today's Verse

Lord teach me to...

I am thankful for...

Prayer Requests

Today's Verse

Lord teach me to...

I am thankful for...

Prayer Requests

DATE

Today's Verse

Lord teach me to...

I am thankful for...

Prayer Requests

DATE

Today's Verse

Lord teach me to...

I am thankful for...

Prayer Requests

DATE

Today's Verse

Lord teach me to...

I am thankful for...

Prayer Requests

Today's Verse

Lord teach me to...

I am thankful for...

Prayer Requests

BE

anxious

FOR NOTHING

Today's Verse

Lord teach me to...

I am thankful for...

Prayer Requests

Today's Verse

Lord teach me to...

I am thankful for...

Prayer Requests

Today's Verse

Lord teach me to...

I am thankful for...

Prayer Requests

DATE

Today's Verse

Lord teach me to...

I am thankful for...

Prayer Requests

Today's Verse

Lord teach me to...

I am thankful for...

Prayer Requests

DATE

Today's Verse

Lord teach me to...

I am thankful for...

Prayer Requests

Today's Verse

Lord teach me to...

I am thankful for...

Prayer Requests

Today's Verse

Lord teach me to...

I am thankful for...

Prayer Requests

Today's Verse

Lord teach me to...

I am thankful for...

Prayer Requests

DATE

Today's Verse

Lord teach me to...

I am thankful for...

Prayer Requests

Today's Verse

Lord teach me to...

I am thankful for...

Prayer Requests

❤ ✕ ❤ ✕ ♥ ✕ ♥

DATE

Today's Verse

Lord teach me to...

I am thankful for...

Prayer Requests

FOR EVERYTHING THERE IS A

season

Today's Verse

Lord teach me to...

I am thankful for...

Prayer Requests

♥ X ♥ X ♥ X ♥

Today's Verse

Lord teach me to...

I am thankful for...

Prayer Requests

❤ X ❤ X ❤ X ❤

DATE

Today's Verse

Lord teach me to...

I am thankful for...

Prayer Requests

Today's Verse

Lord teach me to...

I am thankful for...

Prayer Requests

❤ X ♥ X ♥ X ♥

DATE

Today's Verse

Lord teach me to...

I am thankful for...

Prayer Requests

Today's Verse

Lord teach me to...

I am thankful for...

Prayer Requests

❤ ✕ ❤ ✕ ❤ ✕ ❤

DATE

— Today's Verse —

— Lord teach me to... —

— I am thankful for... —

— Prayer Requests —

DATE

Today's Verse

Lord teach me to...

I am thankful for...

Prayer Requests

DATE

Today's Verse

Lord teach me to...

I am thankful for...

Prayer Requests

Today's Verse

Lord teach me to...

I am thankful for...

Prayer Requests

DATE

Today's Verse

Lord teach me to...

I am thankful for...

Prayer Requests

Today's Verse

Lord teach me to...

I am thankful for...

Prayer Requests

TAKE

heart

Today's Verse

Lord teach me to...

I am thankful for...

Prayer Requests

DATE

Today's Verse

Lord teach me to...

I am thankful for...

Prayer Requests

Today's Verse

Lord teach me to...

I am thankful for...

Prayer Requests

❤ X ❤ X ❤ X ❤

DATE

Today's Verse

Lord teach me to...

I am thankful for...

Prayer Requests

Today's Verse

Lord teach me to...

I am thankful for...

Prayer Requests

❤ ✕ ❤ ✕ ❤ ✕ ❤

DATE

Today's Verse

Lord teach me to...

I am thankful for...

Prayer Requests

─── Today's Verse ───

─ Lord teach me to... ─

─ I am thankful for... ─

── Prayer Requests ──

❤ ✗ ❤ ✗ ❤ ✗ ❤

DATE

Today's Verse

Lord teach me to...

I am thankful for...

Prayer Requests

Today's Verse

Lord teach me to...

I am thankful for...

Prayer Requests

❤ X ❤ X ❤ X ❤

DATE

Today's Verse

Lord teach me to...

I am thankful for...

Prayer Requests

Today's Verse

Lord teach me to...

I am thankful for...

Prayer Requests

Today's Verse

Lord teach me to...

I am thankful for...

Prayer Requests

DATE

Today's Verse

Lord teach me to...

I am thankful for...

Prayer Requests

Today's Verse

Lord teach me to...

I am thankful for...

Prayer Requests